Kids Jokes - Stampy Edition Vol 1 and 2

JOHN JESTER

Following on from the success of *99 Kids Jokes – Stampy Edition Vol 1* and *99 Kids Jokes – Stampy Edition Vol 2*, you can now enjoy both volumes in one convenient edition. It is the ultimate compendium of hilarious jokes based on Stampy's favourite game.

What do Snow Golems wear on their head?
Why won't Endermen eat clowns?
Why don't Guardians eat penguins?

Find out the answers to these and many more hysterical jokes. You will never be able to play the game, without laughing out loud, ever again.

VOLUME ONE

1. How do Creepers like their spawn eggs?

- Terri-fried!

2. What do you call Stampy's Pig that knows karate?

- A pork chop!

3. How many tickles does it take to make Squid laugh?

- Ten-tickles!

4. Why don't Spawn Eggs tell jokes?

- They'd crack each other up!

5. What do Snow Golems wear on their head?

- Ice caps!

6. If Stampy had 2 pet Wolves, he'd call them One and Two, coz if One died, he'd still have Two!

7. What do you call Stampy's Pig thief?

- Ham-burglar!

8. Did you hear about the Creeper's party?

- It was a blast!

9. What kind of music does a Sandstone Block like?

- Rock music!

10. What do you call Stampy's undercover Spider?

- A spy-der!

11. Why can't Stampy's Skeletons play church music?

- Because they have no organs!

12. Why won't Endermen eat clowns?

- They taste funny!

13. What do you get when you cross Stampy's cow with a trampoline?

- A milkshake!

14. What do you get from a Wither Skeleton?

- As far away as possible!

15. Why did half of Stampy's Chicken cross the road?

- To get to his other side!

16. Why was Stampy running around his bed?

- He wanted to catch up on his sleep!

17. What has four legs and goes "Oom, Oom"?

- Stampy's cow walking backwards!

18. What does an Ender Dragon become after it's one year old?

- Two years old!

19. Knock, knock.
- Who's there?
Stampy's cows say.
- Stampy's cows say who?
**No silly, Stampy's cows say
moo!**

**20. What 7 letters did Stampy
say when he opened the chest and
found it empty?**

- O I C U R M T!

**21. What kind of balls do Blazes
play soccer with?**

- Fireballs!

22. How do you spot a modern Cave Spider?

- He doesn't have a web, he has a website!

23. Which side of Stampy's chicken has more feathers?

- The outside!

24. What did Stampy's wolf say when he stepped on its foot?

- Aoooowwwwww!

25. What is Stampy's rabbit's favourite music?

- Hip hop!

26. What is a Zombie's least favourite room in Stampy's house?

- The living room!

27. What would you call Stampy's pet sheep if it had no legs?

- A cloud!

28. Why did Stampy's chicken cross the playground?

- To get to the other slide!

29. What do you get when you cross a mouse with Squid?

- An eektopus!

30. How does a Snow Golem travel to the portal?

- By icicle!

31. Stampy's pet wolf, Minton, ate all my shuttlecocks.

- Bad Minton!

32. What do you call Stampy's chicken in a shellsuit?

- An egg!

33. What do you get if you lay face down under Stampy's cow?

- A pat on the back!

34. What are the smallest rooms in Stampy's house?

- Mushrooms!

35. What makes Stampy's chickens laugh?

- A Comedi-hen!

36. Why don't Guardians eat penguins?

- They can't get the wrappers off!

37. Stampy put on a clean pair of socks every morning for a week.

- By Friday he could hardly put his shoes on!

38. What do Stampy's sheep do on sunny days?

- Have a baa - baa – cue!

39. What is a Zombie's favourite toy?

- A DEADY bear!

40. What has four legs and says OOM?

- Stampy's cow walking backwards!

41. Where do Stampy's sheep get their wool cut?

- At the BAAAbars!

42. What would happen if Pigmen could fly?

- The price of bacon would go up!

43. Why did Stampy's cow cross the road?

- To get to the udder side!

44. Where do you go to buy Zombies?

- The monSTORE!

45. What do Snow Golems like for dessert?

- I scream!

46. Why did the Creeper eat a Torch?

- He wanted a light lunch!

47. How many Pumpkin Seeds can you put in an empty chest?

- One! After that its not empty!

48. Where do Stampy's sheep go on holiday?

- The baaaahamas!

49. What did Stampy's pig say when he was sick?

- Call the ham-bulance!

50. What clothes does Stampy's house wear?

- Ad-dress!

51. Doctor, I feel like Stampy's pig.

How long have you felt like this?

About a weeeeeeek!

52. Who is a Snow Golem's favourite aunt?

- Aunt-artica

53. What time do Zombies wake up?

- At ATE o'clock!

54. What do you call an Iron Golem with no eyes?

- Ron Golem!

55. What day do Spawn Eggs hate most?

- Fry-day!

56. What's in the middle of an Ender Portal?

-The letter E!

57. What kind of make-up do Zombies wear?

- Mas-SCARE-a!

58. What newspaper does Stampy's cow read?

- The evening Moos!

59. What's brown, sounds like a bell, and comes out of a Stampy's cow backwards?

- Dung

**60. Knock Knock
Who's there?
Coal Mine.
Coal Mine who?
Coal Mine number and find out!**

61. What part of the minecart is the laziest?

- The wheels, because they are always tired!

62. What do you get when you cross a Zombie and Stampy's cat?

- A scaredy cat!

63. What did the Torch say to the other Torch?

- I'm going out tonight!

64. Why did Stampy's cookie go to the doctor?

- It was feeling crumby!

65. What do you call a Snow Golem in the desert?

- Lost!

66. Stampy is good friends with 25 letters of the alphabet.

- He doesn't know why!

67. There were two of Stampy's cows in a field. One said "moo", the other one said, "I was going to say that!"

68. What does Stampy's pig put on when it hurts itself?

- Oink-ment

69. What goes ha, ha, ha, clonk?

- An enderman laughing his head off!

70. What's a Ghast's favourite country?

- The Nether-Lands!

71. Where do Snow Golems keep their money?

- In snow banks!

72. How good is Stampy's favourite game?

- Top-Notch!

73. Why did Stampy call his Pig Ink?

- Because it kept running out of the pen!

74. Why did the Creeper cross the road?

- To get to the other Ssssssssside!

75. What's the difference between Stampy and a book?

- You can shut a book up!

76. Where does Stampy take his Minecraft Pigs on Saturday afternoons?

- To the pig-nic!

77. A Skeleton walks into a bar and says, "Pint of cola and a mop!"

78. What happened when the Cave Spider got a new Minecart?

- It took it for a spin!

79. How does a Skeleton call his friends?

- On the tele-bone!

80. What should you do to a blue creeper?

- Cheer it up!

81. What's Stampy's pig's favourite game?

- Pig-pong

82. What do you call an Enderman with no arms or legs floating in a lake?

- Bob

83. Where does a Magma Cube sleep?

- Anywhere he wants to!

84. When do Zombies go to sleep?

- When they are dead tired!

85. Why did the Zombie visit Stampy in hospital?

- He wanted to learn some SICK jokes!

86. Why did Stampy get rid of his Chickens?

- Because they used fowl language!

87. What kind of fish did the Ghast catch?

- Spookled trout!

88. What do you get when you drop a Minecraft Pumpkin?

- Squash!

89. When is the only time a Zombie can make a Snow Golem?

- In the dead of Winter!

90. What do you call a Skeleton that won't do any housework at Stampy's house?

- Lazy-bones!

91. What game does Stampy's cow play at parties?

- Moo-sical chairs!

92. What did Stampy say to the Mushroom?

- You're a fun-guy!

93. What happened after the Creeper went to the French cheese factory?

- All that was left was de brie.

94.Teacher: "Stampy,what do Chickens give you?"
Stampy: "Eggs!"
Teacher: "Now what do Pigs give you?"
Stampy: "Porkchops!"
Teacher: "Great! And what does the Cow give you?"
Stampy: "Homework!"

95. Did you hear about the Villager with a broken left arm and broken left leg?

- Don't worry. He's all-RIGHT now!

96. How would Stampy's trees access the internet?

- They log-in!

97. What do Minecarts eat on their toast?

- Traffic jam!

98. What happens when you cross an Enderman with Stampy's cow?

- I don't know, but I wouldn't milk it!

99. What did the Villager say to the purple Creeper?

- Breathe stupid!

VOLUME TWO

1. What letter is part of Stampy's head?

- 'I'!

2. What kind of trees do skeletons like best?

- Ceme-trees!

3. What do zombie villagers put on their hair?

- Scare-spray!

4. What kind of fish do you find in Stampy's bird cage?

- A perch!

5. How do you make a skeleton laugh?

- Tickle its funny bone!

6. What does a wolf say on Halloween?

- Happy HOWLoween!

7. What can't you give a headless guardian?

- A headache!

8. What's the first thing ghasts do when they get in a minecart?

- The boo-kle their seat belts!

9. Where does a zombie villager eat his lunch?

- At the casket-eria!

10. Why did the skeleton play the piano?

- Because he didn't have any organs!

11. Who won the zombie war?

- It was dead even!

12. What kind of bone should you not give to Stampy's pet wolf?

- A trombone!

13. What do you get if you cross a gangster with a hostile mob?

- Organised slime!

14. Why did the cave spider cross the road?

- To prove he wasn't chicken!

15. What do you call a one inch zombie?

- Tomb Thumb!

16. How does Stampy make his tissue dance?

- Puts a little boogie in it!

17. What do you get when you cross a pig and a cactus?

- A porky-pine!

18. What did the zombie say to Stampy at the coffee shop?

- Scream or sugar!

19. Why did the sheep say "moo"?

- It was learning a new language!

20. Why did the chicken cross the road twice?

- Because it was a double crosser!

21. Why did Stampy take a pencil to bed?

- To draw the curtains!

22. How do zombies tell their future?

- With their HORRORscope!

23. What did the skeleton order for dinner?

- Spare ribs!

24. What kind of bird does Stampy use to lift his blocks?

- A crane!

25. How can you carry water in a sieve?

- Make it into an ice block!

26. What did the coal block say to the iron block?

- Nothing. Coal blocks cannot talk!

27. What do ghasts use to clean their hair?

- Sham-boo!

28. Why are spiders good swimmers?

- They have webbed feet!

29. What did Snow White call her chicken?

- Egg white!

30. How do you mend a broken pumpkin?

- With a pumpkin patch!

31. Why did the snow golem call his wolf Frost?

- Because Frost bites!

32. Stampy wanted to marry a ghast.

- I don't know what possessed him!

33. What do you get when you throw a piano down a mine shaft?

- A flat miner!

34. Did you hear the story about Stampy's broken pencil?

- Never mind. It's pointless!

35. How many rotten eggs does it take to make a stink bomb?

- A phew!

36. What do you get if you cross a motorbike with Stampy's joke book?

- A Yamahahaha!

37. Where do boats go when they are feeling ill?

- To the docs!

38. What do you get if you cross Bambi with a ghast?

- Bamboo!

39. What's big, scary, and has three wheels?

- A slime riding a tricycle!

40. What did the doctor say to the skeleton?

- Aren't you a little late?

41. What time do zombies wake up?

- At ate o'clock!

42. Why did Stampy jump up and down before he drank his juice?

- The carton said to shake well before drinking!

43. How do you keep Stampy busy for hours?

- Give him a piece of paper with 'Please turn over' written on both sides!

44. What happened when the cow jumped over the barbed wire?

- It was an udder catastrophe!

45. How do endermen have a bath with no water?

- They sunbathe!

46. Where can you find a zombie eating plants?

- In a vegetarian restaurant!

47. What happened at the blaze's wedding party?

- They toasted the bride and groom!

48. What do wither skeletons put on their bagels?

- Scream cheese!

49. Why did the zombie bring toilet paper to the party?

- Because he was a party pooper!

50. Why does Stampy like to tickle his horse?

- He gets a big kick out of it!

51. Where do pigs go when they lose their tails?

To the retail store!

52. Who won the skeleton beauty contest?

- No body!

53. Where did the ghast go on vacation?

- The BOO-hamas!

54. How did Stampy cure his headache?

- He put his head through a window and the pane just disappeared!

55. What do you say to Stampy driving his minecart with no redstone?

- How's it going?

56. What's red and red and red all over?

- A spotty mooshroom with sunburn!

57. What goes tick, tock, tick, tock, woof?

- Stampy's watchdog!

58. Why don't pigs make good minecart drivers?

- They are road hogs!

59. How do minecarts hear?

- Through their engine-ears!

60. How do zombies travel on holiday?

- On a scare plane!

61. How do you know eating carrots is good for your eyes?

- Have you ever seen a rabbit wearing spectacles?

62. Who brings a zombie's baby?

- Franken-stork!

63. Why is the letter K like a pig's tail?

- Because it's the end of Pork!

64. When you take away 2 letters from this 5-letter word, you are left with 1. What is it?

- Stone!

65. What follows a skeleton horse wherever he goes?

- His tail of course!

66. Why did the one-handed pig farmer cross the road?

- To get to the second-hand shop!

67. If twenty endermen chase Stampy, what time is it?

- Twenty after one!

68. What does a zombie villager eat with cheese?

- Pickled organs!

69. Where do ghasts go when they want a swim?

- The dead sea!

70. What do you call a haunted chicken?

- A poultry-geist!

71. What's the best way to talk to a spider jockey?

- From afar!

72. What is a ghast's favourite dessert?

- Boo-berry pie!

73. Where should a 500 pound silverfish go?

- On a diet!

74. What should you do with a green slime?

- Wait until its ripe!

75. What is the radius of a pumpkin?

- Pi!

76. What do you get when two skeletons dance in a chest?

- Noise!

77. What is worse than being a three hundred pound spider jockey?

- Being the spider!

78. What is a ghast's favourite party game?

- Hide and shriek!

79. What are spiders webs good for?

- Spiders!

80. What do you call two young married spiders?

- Newly webs!

81. What kind of horses do ghasts like to ride?

- Night-mares!

82. What medicine do zombie villagers take for colds?

- Coffin drops!

83. Why did the minecart stop when it saw a ghast?

- It had a nervous breakdown!

84. How does Stampy count his cows?

- With a Cow-culator!

85. What is invisible and smells like carrots?

- A rabbit fart!

86. Do zombies eat pumpkins with their fingers?

- No, they eat the fingers separately!

87. The past, present and future walk into Stampy's house.

- It was tense!

88. How are zombie villagers like computers?

- They use megaBITES!

89. What do you call a cow with a twitch?

- Beef jerky!

90. Why did Stampy take a ruler to bed?

- He wanted to see how long he slept!

91. Where do zombies go on cruises?

- The DEADiterranean Sea!

92. Stampy walked into a bar.

- Ouch!

93. Why was Stampy staring so hard at his orange juice?

- Because the carton said concentrate.

94. Why does Stampy always walk with his right foot first?

- Because when he puts one foot forward the other is left behind!

95. What do you call a song sung in a minecart?

- A cartoon (car tune)!

96. What do you get when you cross a cement mixer and a chicken?

- A brick layer!

97. Stampy, Amy Lee and L'for lee are stranded in the End and find a genie lamp. The genie grants them each one wish. Amy Lee wishes she was back home, and poof, she is back home. L'for lee wishes the same thing, and poof, he is back home. Stampy, feeling lonely, has his wish. "I'm lonely. Can I have my friends back?"

98. Why did Stampy want a job at the bakery?

- So he could loaf around!

99. What did the mommy ghast say to the baby ghast?

- Don't spook until you're spoken to!

Printed in Great Britain
by Amazon.co.uk, Ltd.,
Marston Gate.